Seven kids live in a shack with Mum.

Mum tells the kids, "Do not let the fox in."

Mum is at the shop.

5

6

7

But it is not Mum. It is the fox, with a big sack.

The fox puts six kids in his sack.
But Ken kid is in a box.

The fox sets off with his sack.
Ken kid runs.

The fox has a nap. Ken runs
to the shop.

Mum and Ken cut the sack.

The six kids run back to
the shack.

Mum and Ken put six rocks in
the sack.

The fox is in his den.

But what is this?